THIS BOOK BELONGS TO

Thank you for buying our Patterns Coloring Book for Children,Teen and Adults!
Inside you will discover more than 100 distinctive Coloring Pages.
These are a mixture of Decorative and Seamless Patterns of nature,animals,life and
much more.

We have personalised the art on single-sided pages. Every image is positioned on its
own page to minimize ink bleed-through to the next design.Different pages are left blank
to prevent ink bleed and to allow removal of pages.

If you will be utilizing markers,we strongly suggest slipping a piece of thick paper or
card paper at the back of the page you're coloring on to help reduce the ink stain on the
next image.

Now Break out your Crayons or Colored pencils!

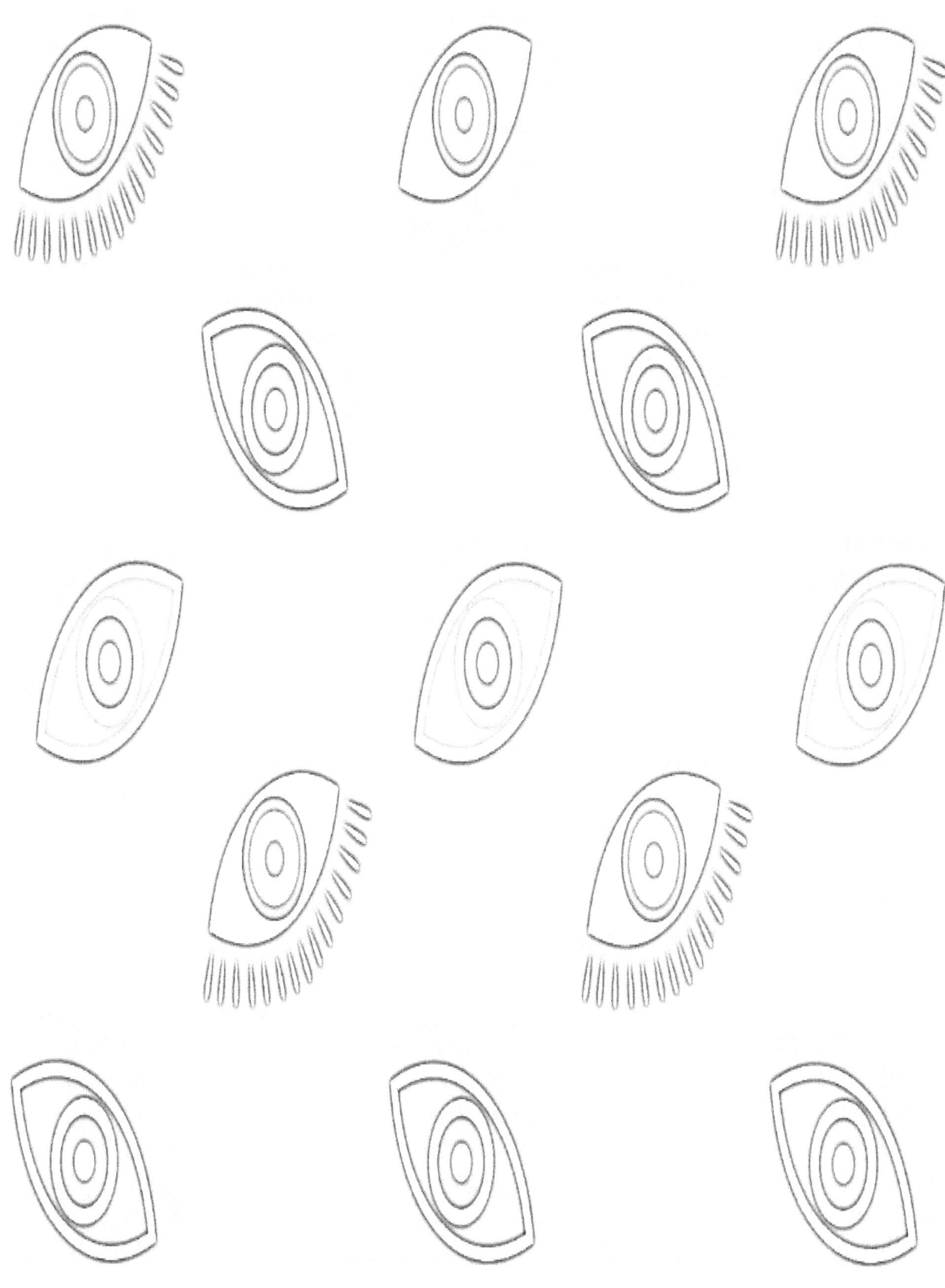

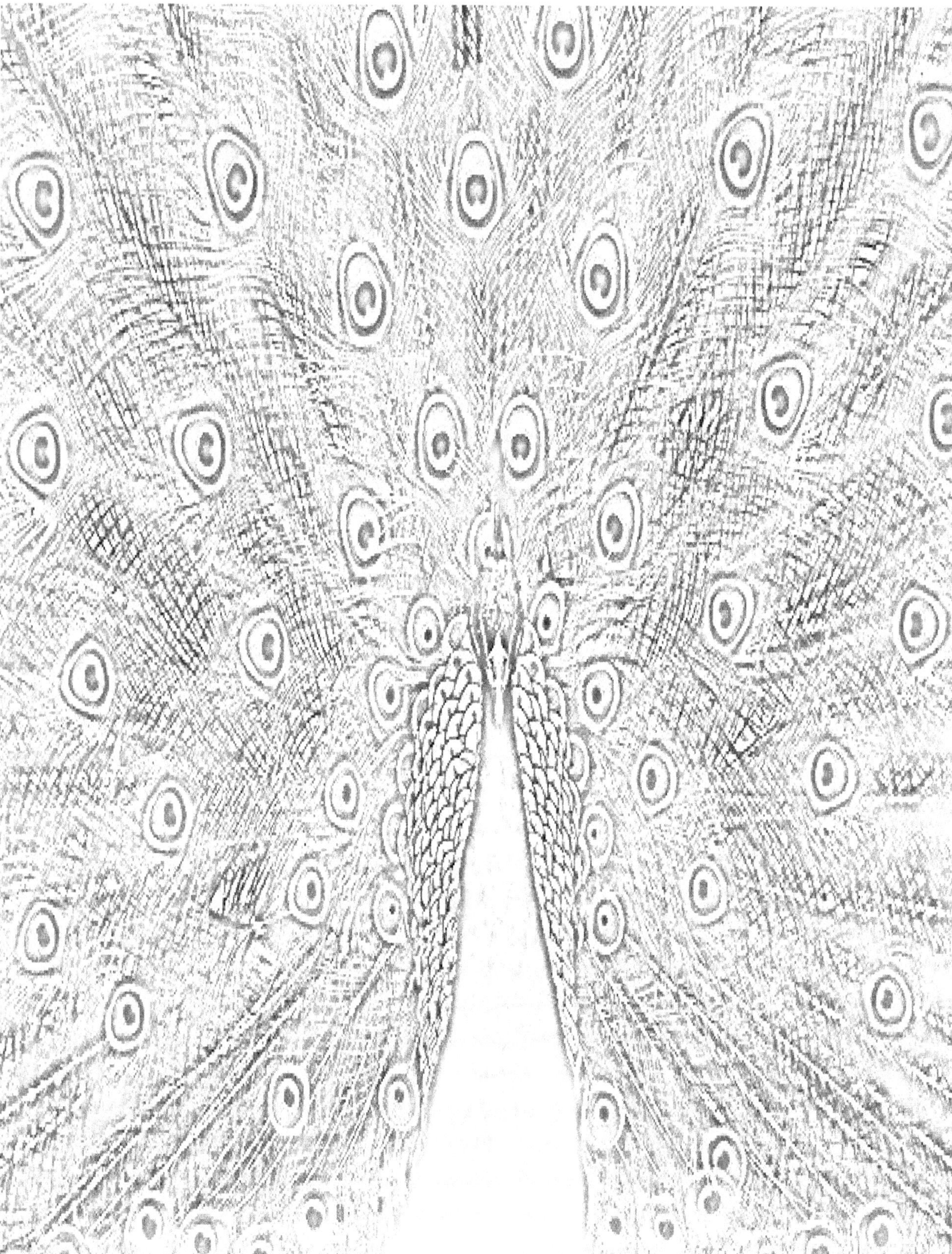

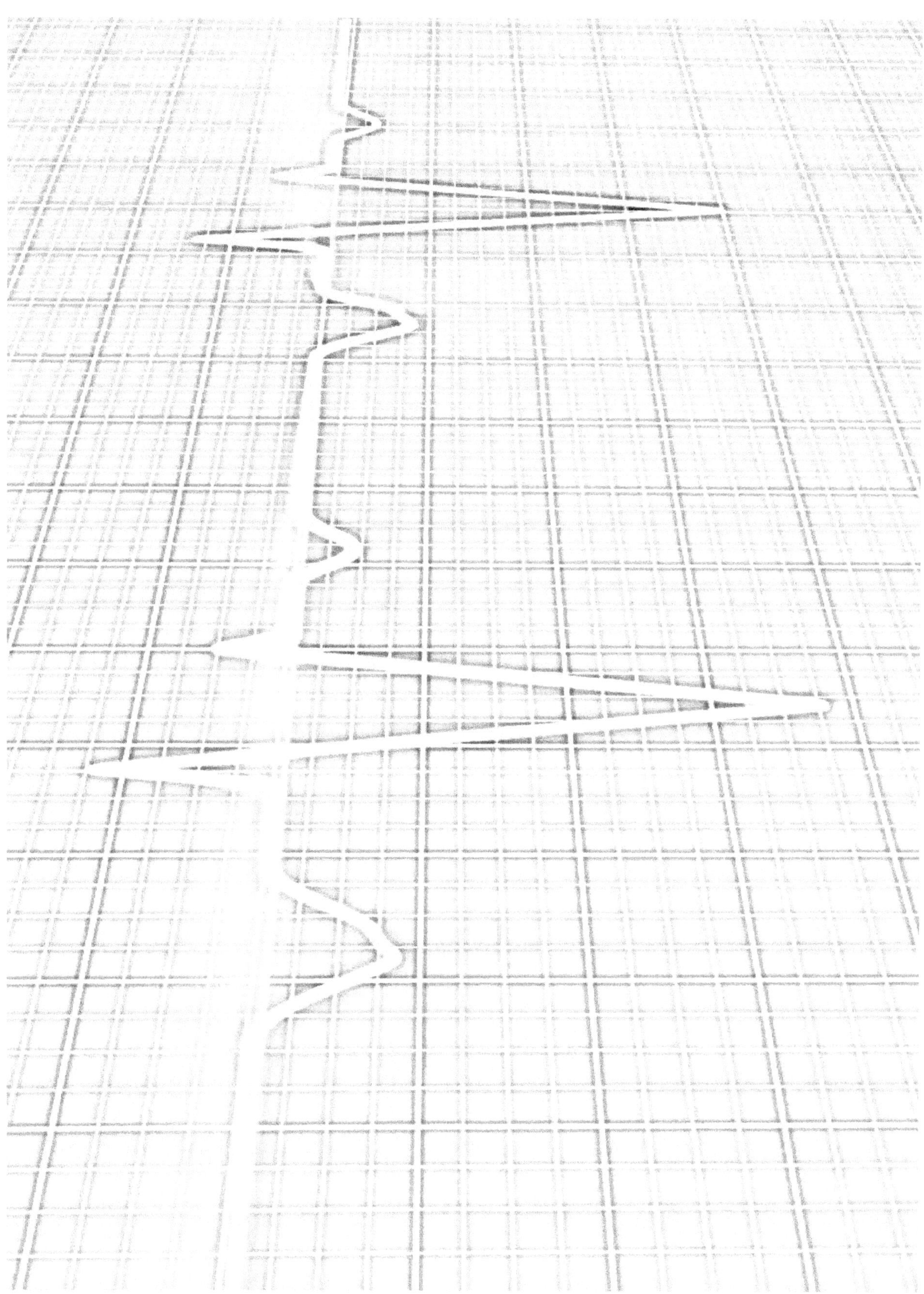

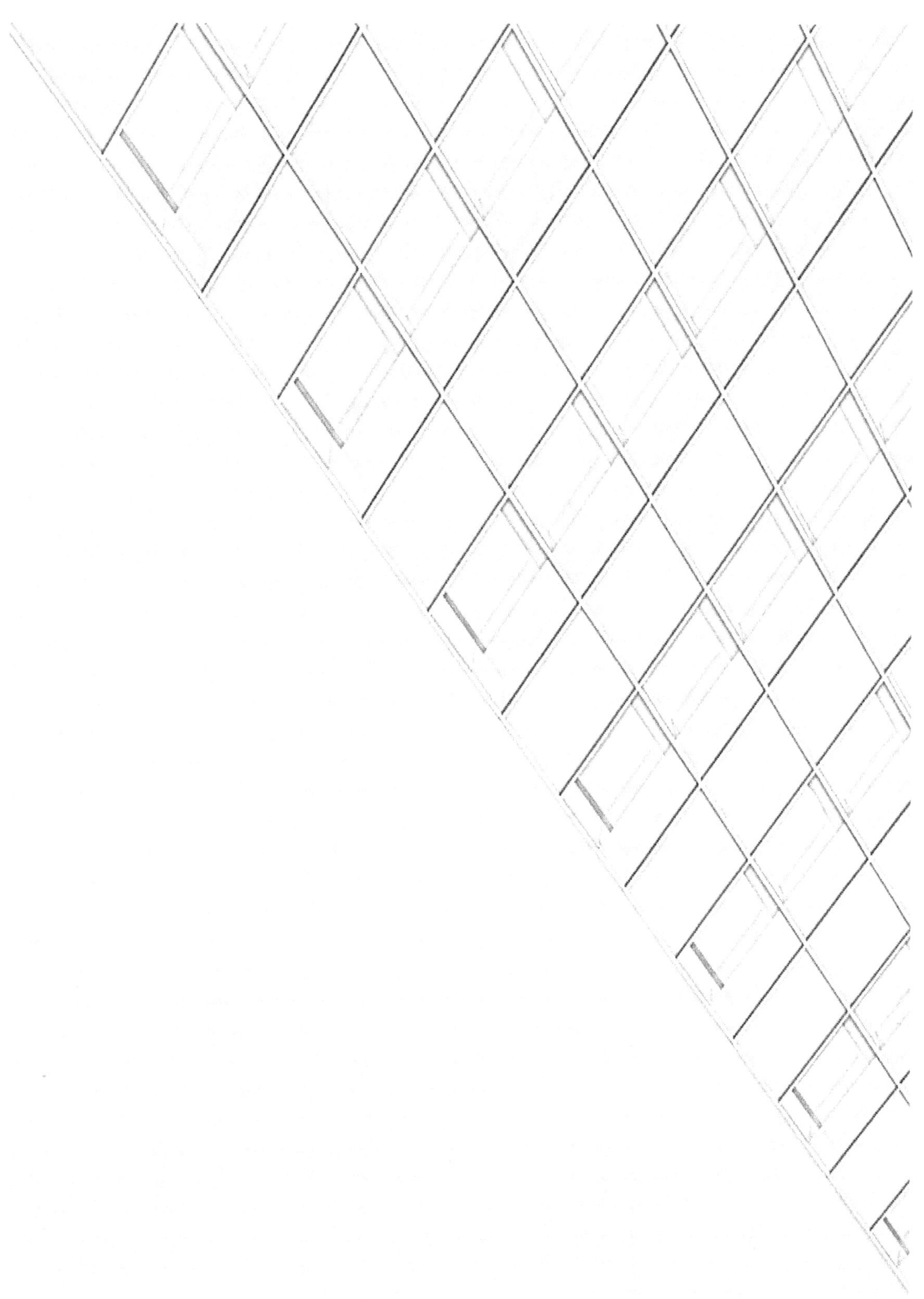

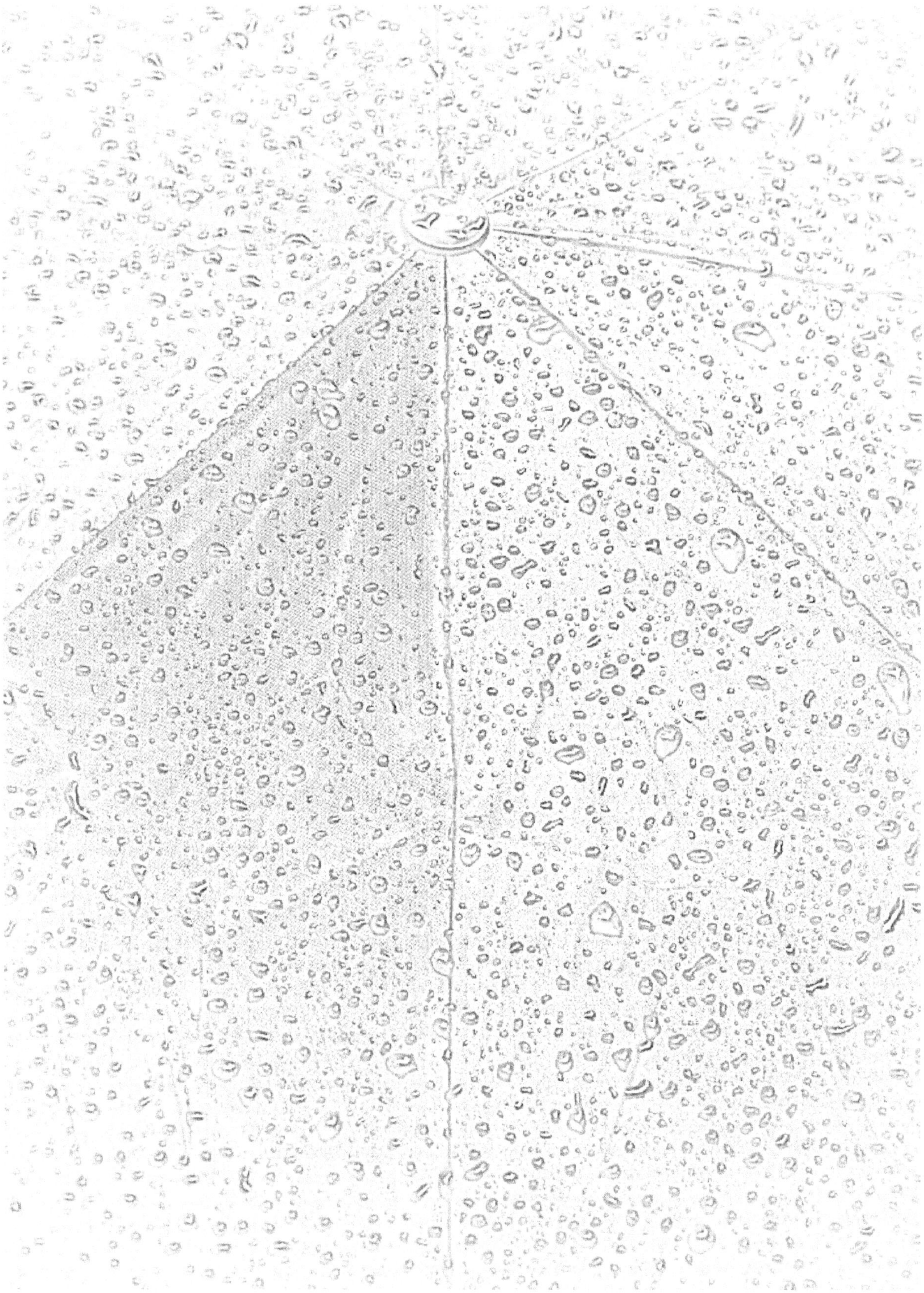

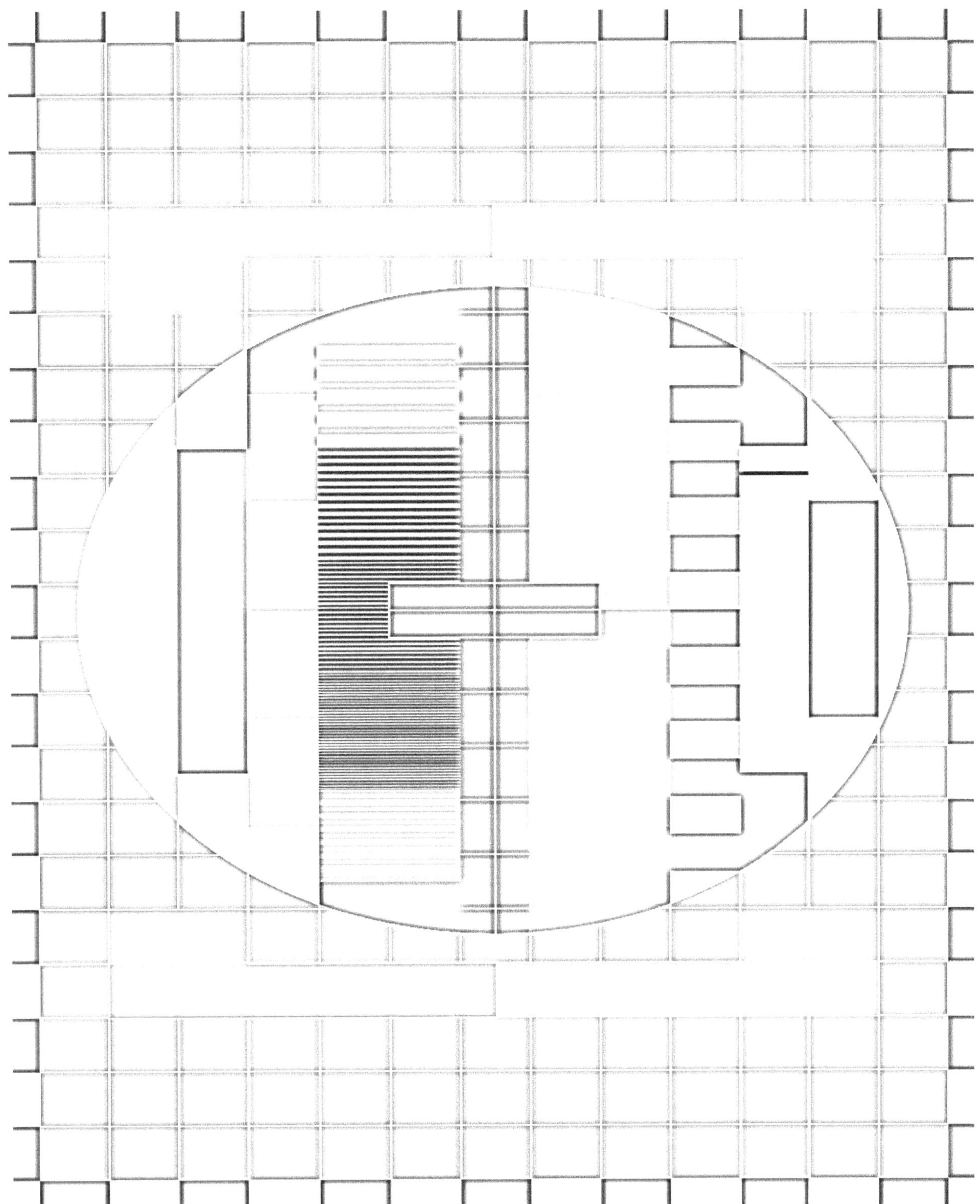

White feathers
White feathers

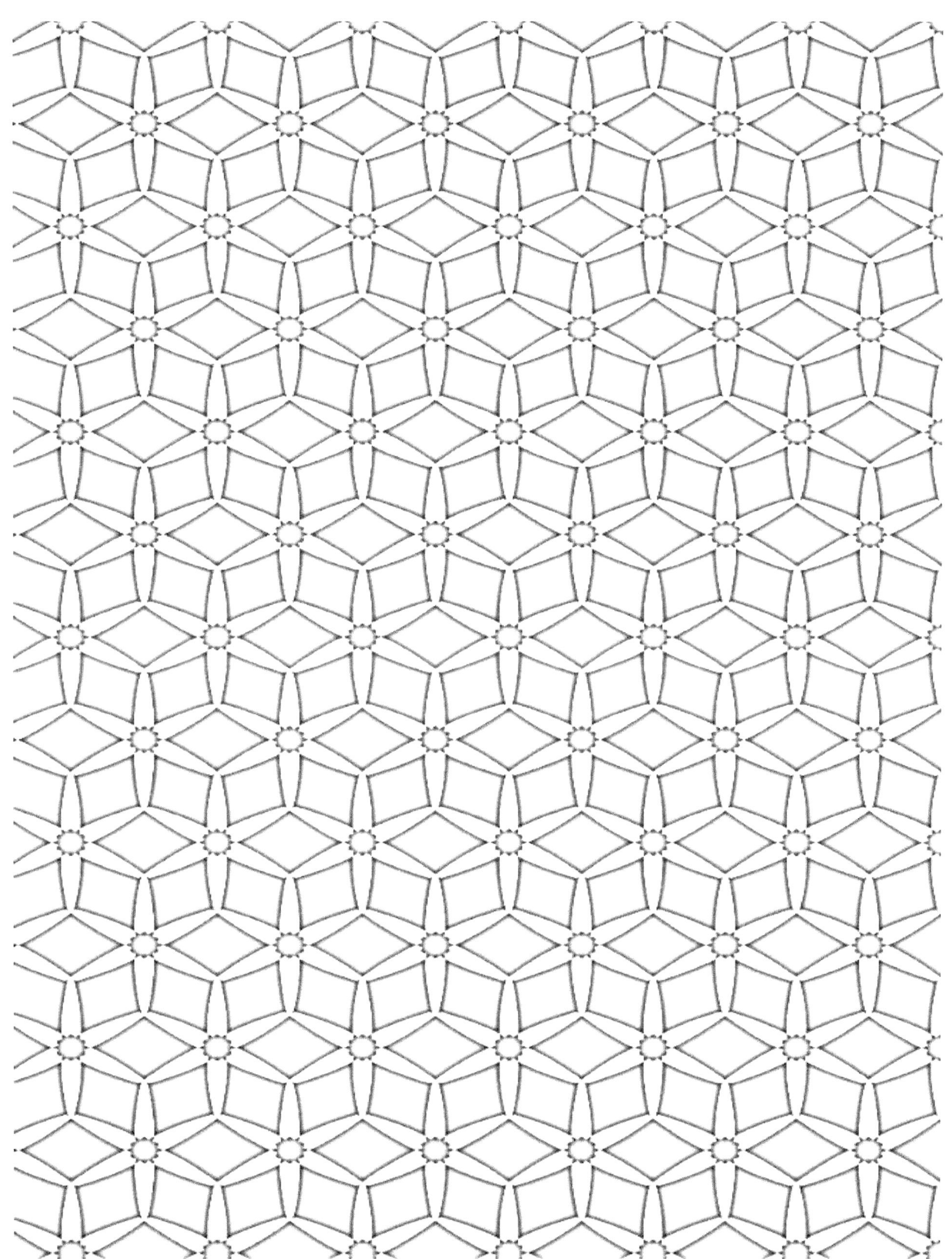

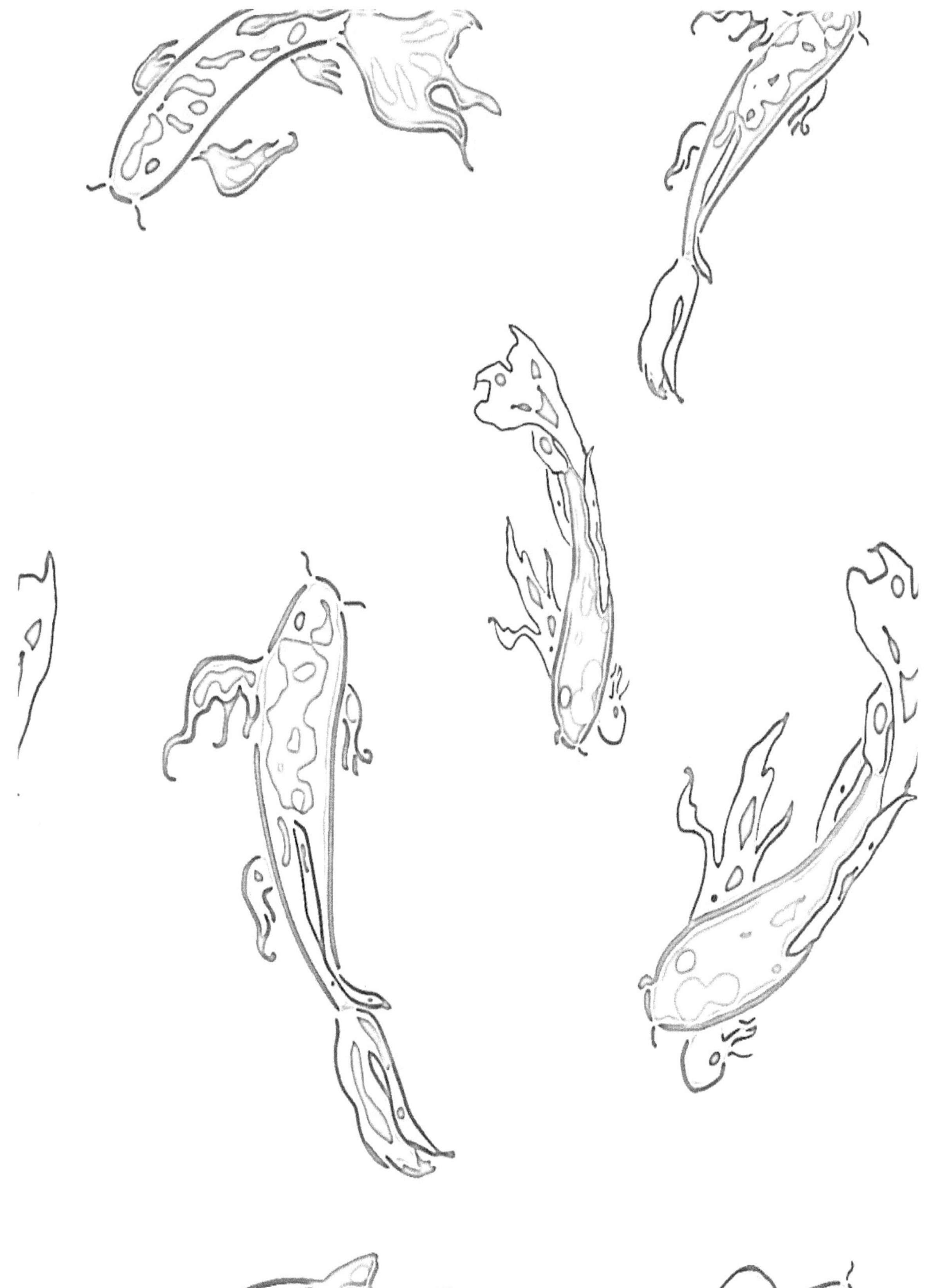

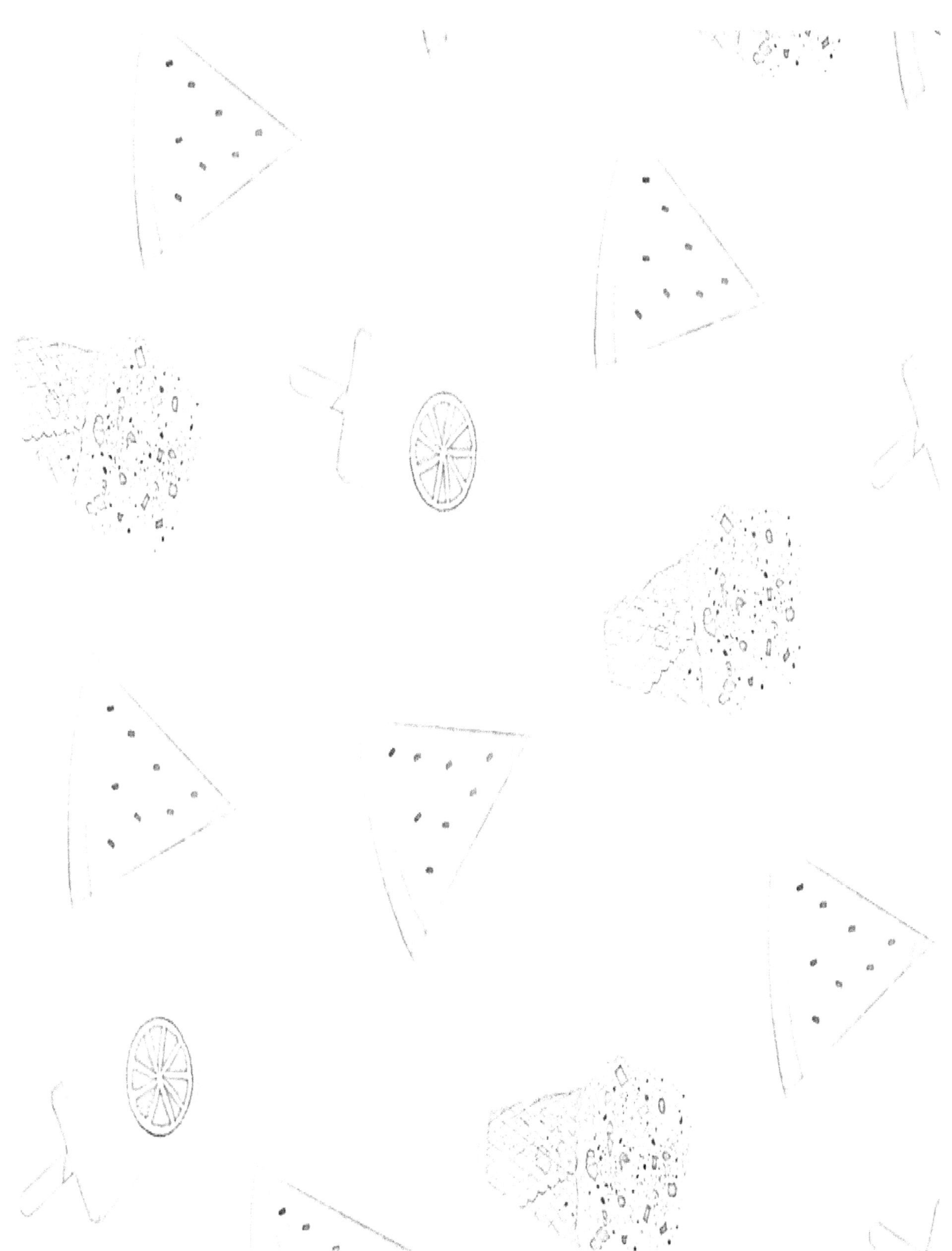

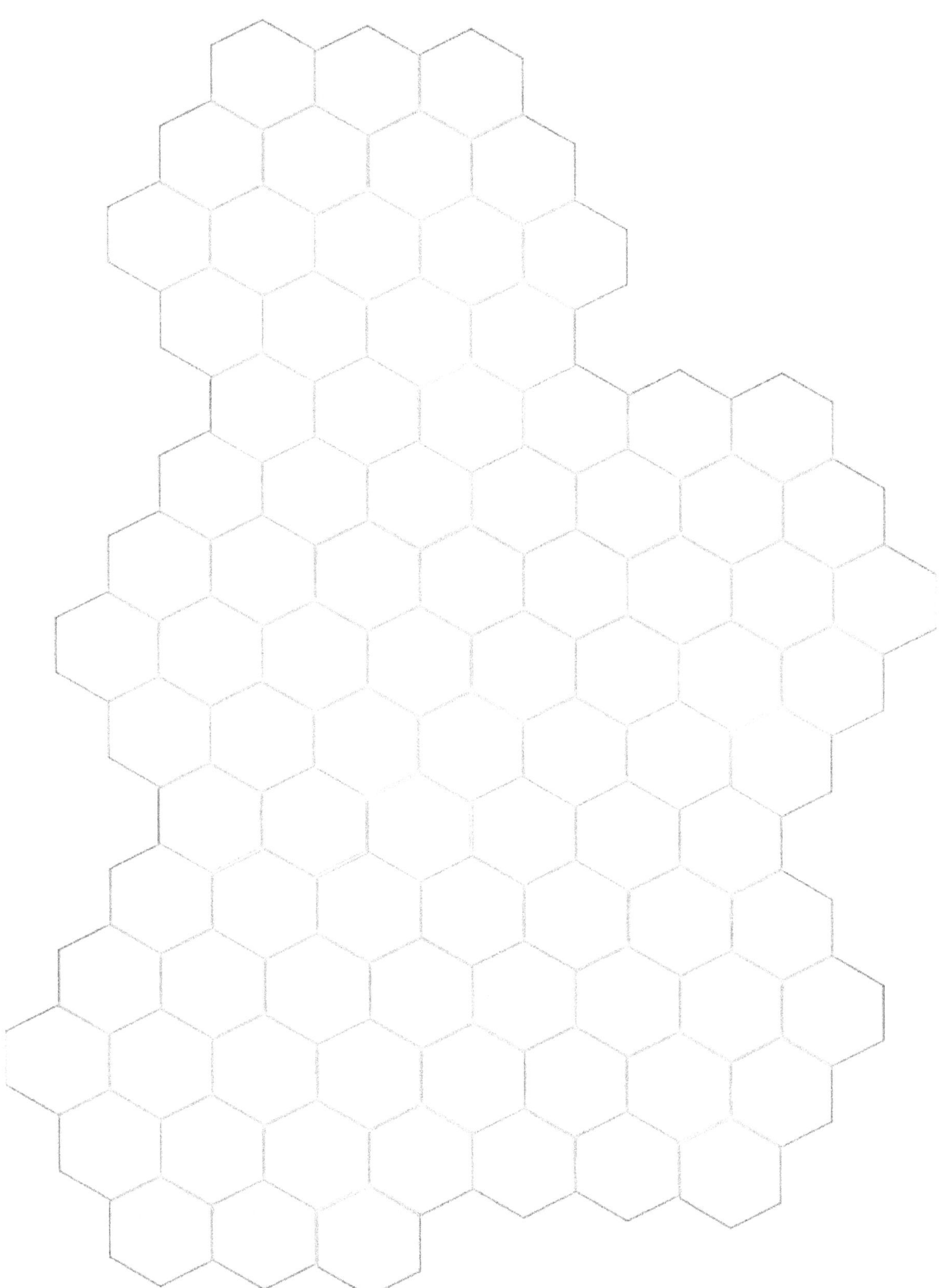

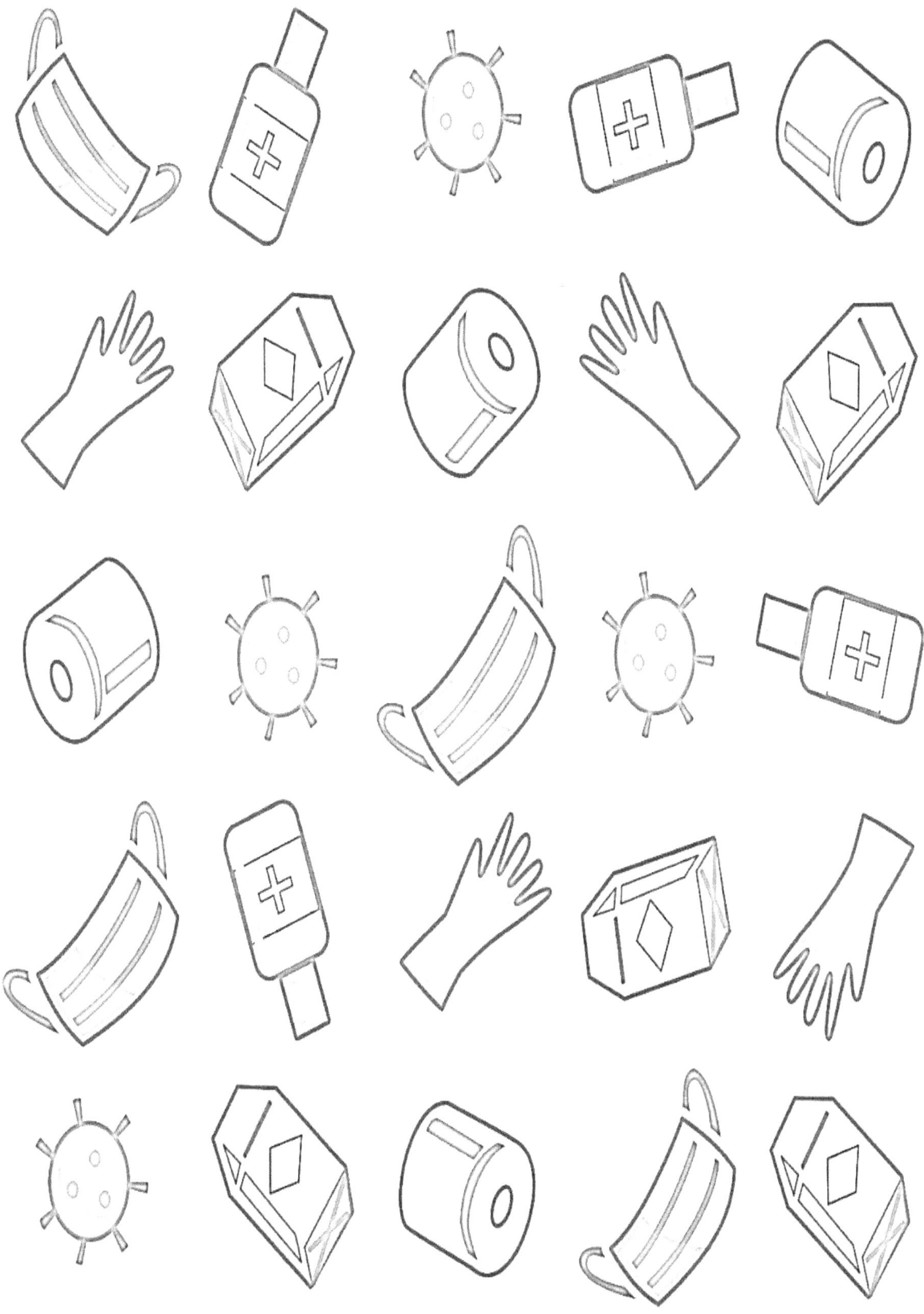

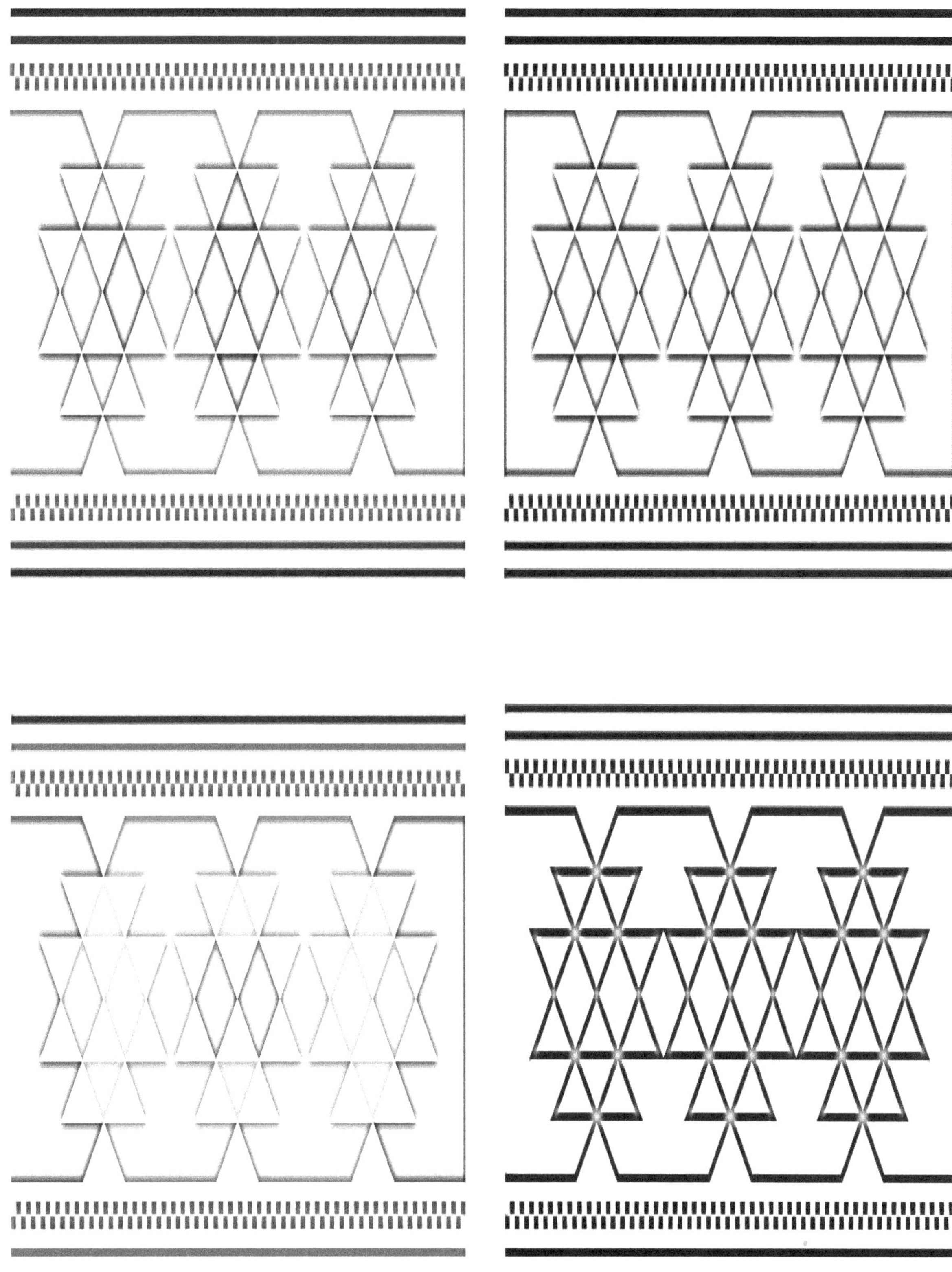

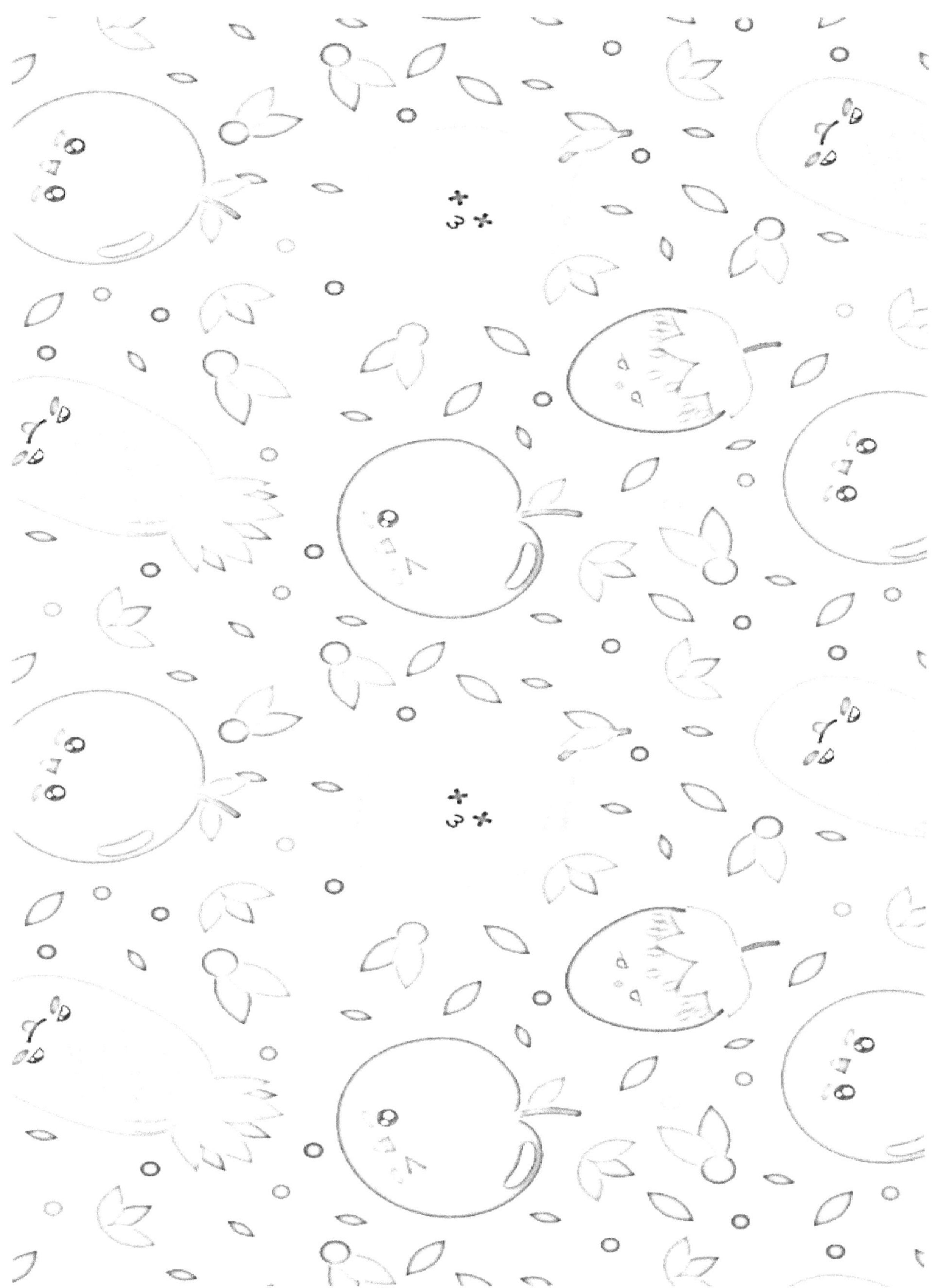

THANK YOU!
ALWAYS BE FREE.